THE POP DIVA QUIZ BOOK

Covering Katy Perry, Lady Gaga, Adele, Kylie
Minogue and Christina Aguilera

Compiled by Chris Cowlin

Unauthorised and Unofficial

First published in 2014 by Apex Publishing Ltd
12A St. John's Road, Clacton on Sea
Essex, CO15 4BP, United Kingdom
www.apexpublishing.co.uk

Please email any queries to Chris Cowlin:
mail@apexpublishing.co.uk

Print layout by
Andrews UK Limited
www.andrewsuk.com

Contents

About the Author

Chris Cowlin is an author, actor and entrepreneur. Born in London in 1980, Chris has achieved a great deal in a short space of time. With a background in printing and advertising, Chris owns a successful publishing company and is himself the author of 120 books. Chris has written on a range of subjects but specialises in football, sport, television and music. His books have been endorsed by many celebrities and sports personalities such as Jonathan Ross, Sir Alex Ferguson, Gary Mabbutt and Gary Lineker. His writing credits include a foreword for a book by notorious criminal, Charles Bronson, who Chris visited in prison on two occasions. He is also a regular contributor to The Sun, Daily Mirror and the letters page of local newspapers.

A keen runner, Chris took part in the London marathon in 2012 and was shortlisted to carry the Olympic Flame in the same year. He regularly competes in running events across the UK and has raised over £35,000 for various charities.

Chris also works as an actor, model and voice over artist. He has been involved in over 200 productions in the last two years including his personal highlight, appearing as an extra in the 2012 James Bond film, Skyfall.

During his career, Chris has appeared in hundreds of newspaper and magazine articles and been interviewed on radio stations across the UK, promoting his books and charity work. He actively participates in social media and has over half a million followers on Twitter.

Chris has been involved in many local community events in recent years; a former local councillor, elected in March 2012, having a majority of 798 votes, beating both the Conservative Party and the Labour Party. He was also a very active school governor between 2010 and 2012.

Chris now lives in London, and has two children, Harry and Aimee.

Visit Chris's website: www.chriscowlin.co.uk or contact him: cowlinchristopher@gmail.com or follow him on Twitter: @ChrisCowlin

THE POP DIVA
QUIZ BOOK

Questions

Katy Perry

1. In which year was Katy born?

2. What is Katy's middle name - Elizabeth, Eileen or Edith?

3. What is Katy's official website address?

4. What nationality is Katy - English, American or Canadian?

5. True or false: Katy was a guest judge on American Idol during 2010?

6. What was the name of Katy's tour, which ran from February until November 2011?

7. Who did Katy marry during October 2010?

8. In which country did Katy get married during October 2010?

9. True or false: Katy was a guest at the Royal Wedding on 29th April 2011, when Prince William married Catherine Middleton?

10. Which single did Katy release in October 2010, reaching number 3 in the UK charts?

11. Which Katy Perry song, released in February 2011 featured Kanye West?

12. Which rapper features in Katy's song 'California Gurls', released in May 2010?

13. What colour dress is Katy wearing on the CD cover of her single 'I Kissed a Girl' released in June 2008?

14. True or false: Perry is Katy's mother's maiden name?

15. How tall is Katy - 5 foot 6 ½ inches, 5 foot 7 ½ inches or 5 foot 8 ½ inches?

16. What was the best UK position in the album charts for Katy's album 'Teenage Dream'?

17. What was Katy's first album called, released in 2001, when she was using her birth name, Katy Hudson?

18. What colour hat is Katy wearing on the front of her 2008 album 'One of the Boys'?

19. What is the name of Katy's fragrance?

20. In which year did Katy win a BRIT award for 'International Female Artist' - 2008, 2009 or 2010?

21. What colour lipstick is Katy wearing on her album cover of 'Teenage Dream'?

22. Who did Katy date up until December 2008, front man of band 'Gym Class Heroes'?

23. In which year was Katy's single 'Teenage Dream' released?

24. What is Katy's song called which appears as track 5 on her album 'Teenage Dream'?

25. True or false: Katy's real Christian name is Katheryn?

26. For which character did Katy provide the voice in the 2011 film The Smurfs?

27. On which UK television show was Katy a guest judge on the seventh series in 2010?

28. How many different outfits did Katy wear during the 2009 MTV Europe Music Awards?

29. Which award did Katy win at the IFPI Platinum Europe Awards in 2009 for her album 'One of the Boys'?

30. Who wrote Katy's song 'Mannequin'?

31. What is Katy holding on the front of her single 'Hot n Cold', released in September 2008?

32. In which country did Katy's album 'One of the Boys' debut at number 10 and peak at number 6?

33. Which of Katy's singles appears on the compilation CD 'Now That's What I Call Music! 72'?

34. Which of Katy's singles won the Single of the Year and the Music Video of the Year awards at the Soul and Jazz Awards in 2011?

35. At which awards show in Australia did Katy wear a dress with an unusual print of a naked woman with a double bass bottom in May 2011?

36. At which number in the FHM Magazine's 100 Sexiest Women did Katy appear in 2010?

37. How many nominations did Katy receive at the MTV Video Music Awards for her song 'I Kissed a Girl' in 2008, failing to win any of them?

38. What number was Katy in a poll on 'Askmen' for being the most desirable women of 2011?

39. What colour glasses was Katy wearing on the front of her single 'Ur So Gay'?

40. From which upscale department store chain in the United States is Katy's fragrance available?

41. True or false: Katy and Snoop Dogg performed 'California Gurls' at the MTV Movie Awards in June 2010?

42. How long does Katy's song 'Peacock' last - 3 minutes 42 seconds, 3 minutes 52 seconds or 4 minutes 2 seconds?

43. What rating out of four stars did Katy's album 'Teenage Dream' receive from USA Today?

44. True or false: Katy's album 'Teenage Dream' was nominated for Album of the Year at the Grammy Awards?

45. What is the tempo of Katy's song 'Firework' - 126 beats per minute, 128 beats per minute or 130 beats per minute?

46. Which American music magazine described Katy's single 'Hot n Cold' as a 'spunky, climate-controlled kiss-off'?

47. True or false: Katy appeared in a commercial for 'Proactiv Solution' acne skin care?

48. Which of Katy's singles, released in 2010, was originally intended for American hip hop group Three 6 Mafia?

49. What is the name of Katy's tour which started in January 2009 and finished in November 2009?

50. Which award did Katy win at the FiFi Awards in 2011 for her fragrance which she released in 2010?

51. What NRJ Music Awards award did Katy win in 2009?

52. True or false: Katy sang her song 'Hot n Cold' in Simlish for the soundtrack of 'Sims 2: Apartment Life'?

53. Which French pop musician supported Katy on her 2009 tour of the United Kingdom?

54. With which American electronic rock group did Katy record a single titled 'Starstrukk', released in 2009?

55. At which number in the UK charts did Katy's single 'Thinking of You' peak - 17, 27 or 37?

56. Where was Katy on tour on 7th and 8th of May 2011?

57. What colour was Katy's hair on the promotional poster for her 2011 tour?

58. Where in the world was Katy's video for 'Firework' shot?

59. For which two Miley Cyrus songs did Katy provide background vocals from the 2008 album 'Breakout'?

60. In which country was Katy touring between 28th April and 5th May 2011?

61. Which record label produced Katy's album 'Katy Perry: MTV Unplugged'?

62. True or false: Katy performed her single 'Firework' on the Late Show with David Letterman in August 2010?

63. At which London night club did Katy appear on 26th and 27th February 2009 whilst on tour in England?

64. What colour is Katy's name on her album 'One of the Boys' released in 2008?

65. Can you name Katy's song that is listed as track 6 on her album 'One of the Boys'?

66. True or false: Katy's song 'I Kissed a Girl' was inspired by Scarlett Johansson?

67. In which shape bottle is Katy's fragrance which she released in November 2010 - a cat, a chocolate or a giraffe?

68. True or false: Katy's mother's aunt and uncle were screenwriter Eleanor Perry and director Frank Perry?

69. For whom did Katy provide the background vocals for his 2008 album 'Wanderlust'?

70. True or false: Katy is a natural blonde, she dyes her hair black?

71. At which number in the Irish charts did Katy's song 'Hot n Cold' peak?

72. Which of Katy's songs did she win the 2008 Virgin Media Music Award for 'Best Track'?

73. What is Katy wearing on the front of her album 'Teenage Dream'?

74. In which position was Katy on Maxim magazine's Hot 100 in the 2010 list?

75. What colour hair does Katy have on the front of her single 'Firework'?

76. On which ABC Family television series did Katy appear during March 2008?

77. True or false: Katy once studied Italian opera?

78. What star sign is Katy?

79. What colour eyes does Katy have?

80. True or false: Katy has German, Portuguese, Irish, and English ancestry?

81. What is the name of track 6 on Katy's album 'Teenage Dream'?

82. Which award did Katy present with Nicki Minaj to Eminem at the 2010 MTV Video Music Awards?

83. In which month during 2009 did Katy get engaged to Russell Brand?

84. True or false: Katy grew up listening to only gospel music and sang in her local church as a child?

85. Which artist produced the painting for Katy's album 'Teenage Dream'?

86. Which of Katy's albums was the first to go to number 1 in the UK album charts?

87. True or false: Katy was a contestant on Celebrity Big Brother in 2010?

88. Which award did Katy win at the Juno Awards in 2011?

89. Which Turkish musician supported Katy on her 2009 tour of Istanbul?

90. On which American day time soap did Katy appear as herself in June 2008, posing for the cover of the June 2008 issue of the fictional magazine Restless Style?

91. How many Kaiet Music Awards did Katy win in 2009 for her single 'I Kissed a Girl'?

92. True or false: Katy won the Best Breakthrough award at the MTV Australia Awards in 2009?

93. What colour lipstick is Katy wearing on the front of her single 'Thinking of You'?

94. In which year did Katy release her single 'Thinking of You'?

95. At which number in the FHM Magazine's 100 Sexiest Women did Katy appear in 2009?

96. Who is Katy's stylist?

97. Who produced Katy's single 'Ur So Gay' released in 2007?

98. What was the name of the episode that Katy appeared in as herself in The Simpsons in 2010?

99. What was Katy's highest chart position in Germany with her single 'Firework'?

100. On which English chat show did Katy perform her single 'Firework' during November 2010?

Lady Gaga

101. In what year was Lady Gaga born in New York City - 1985, 1986 or 1987?

102. What is the name of Lady Gaga's debut studio album, released in August 2008?

103. In what month during 2009 was Lady Gaga's single 'Paparazzi' released?

104. What is the name of track 12 on Lady Gaga's debut album?

105. What is Lady Gaga's real full name?

106. True or false: Lady Gaga won a BRIT Award for Female Solo Artist in 2010?

107. What colour are Lady Gaga's eyes - brown, blue or green?

108. What nationality is Lady Gaga - English, American or Canadian?

109. How old was Lady Gaga when she started to learn to play the piano?

110. In what year did Lady Gaga release her debut studio album 'The Fame'?

111. How many tracks are there on Lady Gaga's album 'The Fame Monster' - 8, 10 or 12?

112. Can you name the Lady Gaga song, released in November 2009 as a digital download only, reaching number 89 in the UK charts?

113. Which single did Lady Gaga release in April 2011?

114. Can you name the April 2009 single that Lady Gaga features on by American rapper Wale?

115. In what month during 2011 did Lady Gaga release the single 'Born This Way'?

116. What are Lady Gaga's two favourite perfumes?

117. True or false: Lady Gaga's father is the owner of a Wi-Fi company in New York City?

118. Which song did Michael Bolton write with Lady Gaga?

119. What musical instrument can Lady Gaga play?

120. True or false: Lady Gaga is a supporter of Tottenham Hotspur Football Club?

121. What star sign is Lady Gaga?

122. What is the name of Lady Gaga's debut single, released in April 2008?

123. How many BRIT awards did Lady Gaga win during 2010?

124. With which record label was Lady Gaga signed to at the age of 19, although she was dropped by the label after only three months?

125. Which Queen song inspired Lady Gaga to use her stage name 'Lady Gaga'?

126. What is Lady Gaga's natural hair colour, is she - a natural brunette, a natural blonde, a natural red head?

127. True or false: As of Spring 2011, the University of South Carolina is running a course titled 'Lady Gaga and the Sociology of the Fame'?

128. What country was Lady Gaga born in?

129. What hand does Lady Gaga write with?

130. At age 11 what is the name of the school that Lady Gaga attended?

131. Which celebrity did Lady Gaga go to school with?

132. In what month during 2011 did Lady Gaga's 'Born this way' album come out?

133. What is Lady Gaga's favourite cartoon character?

134. What is the Christian name of Lady Gaga's mother?

135. True or false: Lady Gaga loves Italian food especially pasta?

136. What is Lady Gaga's favourite book?

137. How many tattoos does Lady Gaga have?

138. What is Lady Gaga's official website?

139. What is the name of the university Lady Gaga attended?

140. Which David Bowie hit is Lady Gaga's all time favourite song?

141. How tall is Lady Gaga - 5 feet 1 inch, 5 feet 4 inches or 5 feet 7 inches?

142. In April 2011 which Lady Gaga song did the Glee cast perform?

143. What is Lady Gaga's favourite television show?

144. True or false: Lady Gaga joined the Pussycat Dolls in May 2009 for an Australian tour?

145. Which artist's baby is Lady Gaga godmother for?

146. Which artist does Lady Gaga collaborate with in the song 'Just Dance'?

147. True or false: Lady Gaga is left handed?

148. What is on the top of Lady Gaga's head in the video 'Poker Face'?

149. What was the dress made of that Lady Gaga wore at the MTV Video Music Awards?

150. How many siblings does Lady Gaga have?

151. How long is Lady Gaga's song 'Bad Romance' (the digital download) - 3 minutes 54 seconds, 4 minutes, 34 seconds or 4 minutes, 54 seconds?

152. What did Lady Gaga appear out of at the Grammys in February 2011?

153. What is the name of the song which she first produced with RedOne?

154. True or false: Lady Gaga's song 'Just Dance', released in April 2008, was a UK number 1?

155. Who is Lady Gaga's favourite actor?

156. What breed of dog is in the video 'Poker Face'?

157. What number in the UK charts did Lady Gaga's song 'Love Game' reach?

158. Why did Lady Gaga dye her hair blonde?

159. True or false: Lady Gaga came out as a bisexual in 2008?

160. On which MTV show did Lady Gaga make a special guest appearance?

161. How many tattoos does Lady Gaga have?

162. True or false: Lady Gaga's song 'Telephone', released in January 2010, was a UK number 1?

163. What are Lady Gaga's two favourite foods?

164. At what hospital was Lady Gaga born?

165. On which TV show did Lady Gaga appear during October 2009 to have a catfight with Madonna?

166. What is Lady Gaga's favourite colour?

167. In what year will Lady Gaga celebrate her 30th birthday?

168. True or false: Lady Gaga's single 'Born This Way' was the fastest selling single in iTunes history, selling over a million copies in five days?

169. What is the date of Lady Gaga's birthday?

170. What colour was Lady Gaga's hair in January 2010?

171. What are Lady Gaga's favourite shoes?

172. How long was Lady Gaga's song 'Eh Eh (Nothing Else I Can Say)' on for - 2 minutes 37 seconds, 2 minutes 57 seconds or 3 minutes 7 seconds?

173. True or false: Lady Gaga attended the 2010 MTV Video Music Awards accompanied by four service members of the United States Armed Forces?

174. What country was Lady Gaga touring in from 27th to 29th November 2009?

175. Who did Lady Gaga write the song 'Born This Way' with?

176. What colour is Lady Gaga's name and the album name 'The Fame Monster' on the CD cover?

177. What is the name of Lady Gaga's tour, which ran from November 2009 until May 2011?

178. Apart from Lady Gaga herself, what else is featured on the cover of her 2011 album 'Born This Way'?

179. True or false: Lady Gaga won the iTunes Award for Best Song for her single 'Telephone' in 2010?

180. What is the name of the first song from Lady Gaga's album 'The Fame Monster'?

181. True or false: Lady Gaga wrote songs for the Pussycat Dolls and Britney Spears?

182. Lady Gaga's song 'Telephone' was originally written for which pop star?

183. True or false: Lady Gaga attended the Royal Wedding, when Prince William married Catherine Middleton on 29th April 2011?

184. Which award did Lady Gaga win at the 2011 TRL Awards?

185. Where did Lady Gaga record her single 'Just Dance' - Hollywood, London or Paris?

186. True or false: Lady Gaga attended an all girls school?

187. In what month during 2010 did Lady Gaga release her single 'Telephone' in the UK?

188. Which Lady Gaga song won 'The Record of the Year' award in the UK during 2009?

189. True or false: Lady Gaga appeared on Big Brother UK in 2010?

190. How long does the video 'Born This Way' by Lady Gaga last for - 6 minutes 45 seconds, 7 minutes 3 seconds or 7 minutes 20 seconds?

191. Which American R&B singer featured on Lady Gaga's single 'Telephone', released in January 2010?

192. True or false: Lady Gaga's song 'Poker Face', released in September 2008, was a UK number 1?

193. Which award did Lady Gaga win at The Q Awards for her single 'Just Dance' in 2009?

194. True or false: Lady Gaga's hair is falling out because she keeps bleaching and dying it blonde?

195. True or false: lady Gaga was named 'The Artist of the Year' for 2010 by Billboard?

196. True or false: Lady Gaga was a contestant on The X Factor in the UK in 2008?

197. What is the name of Lady Gaga's sister?

198. From which album is Lady Gaga's song 'Bad Romance'?

199. True or false: Lady Gaga won the 2011 NME Award for Hero of the Year?

200. For which song did Lady Gaga win a Grammy award during 2010 for the 'Best Dance Recording'?

Adele

201. What is the title of Adele's 2008 album?

202. Which of Adele's singles was released in November 2011 as her album '21's' third official single in the United States?

203. Which of Adele's songs is track 7 on her album '21'?

204. Which song is on the B side of Adele's single 'Rolling in the Deep'?

205. What is the length of Adele's album '19' - 43 minutes 41 seconds, 45 minutes 41 seconds or 47 minutes 41 seconds?

206. Which two awards did Adele win at the 51st Grammy Awards in 2009?

207. In which year during the 1980s was Adele born in Tottenham, London?

208. Which record label produced Adele's song 'Turning Tables'?

209. Which BRIT award did Adele win in 2008?

210. True or false: Adele's first two albums went to number 1 in the UK's album charts?

211. At which position in the charts in Ireland did Adele's song 'Set Fire to the Rain' peak?

212. How tall is Adele - 5 foot 8 inches, 5 foot 9 inches or 5 foot 10 inches?

213. What is Adele's official website address?

214. What is Adele's surname?

215. How many stars did The Observer newspaper give Adele's album '19' - three, four or five?

216. With whom did Adele write the song 'Someone Like You'?

217. What football team does Adele support?

218. True or false: Adele appeared and performed at Goodison Park, the home of Everton Football Club, during October 2011?

219. In which year did Adele release her album '21'?

220. On which TV channel did Adele's music video for 'Rolling in the Deep' premiere during December 2010?

221. True or false: Adele currently lives in Portugal and has done since June 2011?

222. In which month during 2008 did Adele tour Japan?

223. What is Adele sitting on in the photo on the front cover of her single 'Cold Shoulder'?

224. True or false: Adele toured in Barcelona and Madrid on 1 and 2 April 2011?

225. How many weeks, in total, was Adele's first album in the top 100 in the UK's album charts - 70, 74 or 78?

226. True or false: Adele's single 'Make You Feel My Love' spent a total of 68 weeks in the top 100 in the UK charts between October 2008 and November 2011?

227. On 9 August 2011, the opening night of the second North American leg of her 'Adele Live' tour in Vancouver BC, Adele dedicated her performance of her song 'Make You Feel My Love' to which singer who had sadly passed away a few weeks before?

228. Which three BRIT awards was Adele nominated for in 2009?

229. True or false: Adele released her autobiography in 2010 titled Adele: Singing is My Life?

230. At which position in the UK charts did Adele's single 'Chasing Pavements' stay for the first three weeks, during January and February 2008?

231. True or false: On 19 April 2011 Adele's first album was third and her second album was second in the UK's album charts?

232. What is on the B side of her 2008 single 'Cold shoulder'?

233. In which year will Adele celebrate her 30th birthday?

234. True or false: Adele finished her course at the BRIT School for Performing Arts and Technology in Croydon during May 2006, where her classmates included Leona Lewis and Jessie J?

235. What is the longest song on Adele's album '21'?

236. Which American singer cited Adele as one of the influences for her fourth album, titled '4'?

237. True or false: Adele made Billboard history by becoming the first female singer to top the artist, album and singles list in the same year during 2011?

238. Which former Pop Idol winner did Adele support at the 2007 MENCAP Little Noise Sessions, a charity concert at London's Union Chapel?

239. Which of Adele's singles did she perform live on the BBC1 show Friday Night with Jonathan Ross during December 2007?

240. At which venue in Chalk Farm, London, did Adele perform on 21 December 2008?

241. On which BBC1 show was Adele a guest alongside comedian Jack Whitehall and actress Miranda Hart during 2011?

242. True or false: In December 2011, worldwide sales for Adele's album '21' surpassed 16 million copies?

243. At which position in the Hungarian Album Chart did Adele's second album peak - 1, 11 or 21?

244. Where in the world did Adele tour during May 2011?

245. Which single did Adele release in 2010, making it to the number 2 position in the UK singles charts?

246. In which year did Adele first perform on the ITV show Loose Women?

247. Which Urban Music Award did Adele win in 2008?

248. Who wrote Adele's 2008 song 'Make You Feel My Love'?

249. True or false: Adele won the award 'Best Female Artist' at the 2011 BT Digital Music Awards?

250. At which position in the UK charts did Adele's song 'Hometown Glory' peak - 9, 19 or 29?

251. What is the title of track 2 on Adele's debut album?

252. What was the name of Adele's second concert tour in 2011?

253. For how many weeks was Adele's single 'Cold Shoulder' in the top 20 in the UK's singles charts?

254. What is Adele's twitter address?

255. Which award did Adele win in 2011 at the MOBO Awards?

256. In which year did Adele first win the UK Solo Artist of the Year at the Glamour Women of the Year Awards?

257. True or false: Adele underwent throat surgery for a haemorrhaged vocal cord during November 2011?

258. How many Grammy nominations did Adele receive during 2010?

259. Which charity benefitted during September 2009 when Adele performed at the Brooklyn Academy of Music, for the VH1 'Divas' event?

260. In which year did Adele start her tour titled 'An Evening with Adele'?

261. True or false: Adele's single 'Someone Like You' was a number 1 in Australia?

262. Which of Adele's 2011 singles was a number 1 in Belgium, Czech Republic, Netherlands, Poland and Slovakia?

263. Which Jennifer Lopez song knocked Adele's song 'Someone Like You' off the number 1 position in the UK charts on 9 April 2011?

264. True or false: Adele toured Denmark during September 2011?

265. Which ARIA Award was Adele nominated for during 2011?

266. For how many weeks in total did Adele's single 'Someone Like You' spend in the number 1 position in the UK charts?

267. True or false: Adele's single 'Chasing Pavements' was a number 1 in the charts in Norway?

268. How many weeks did Adele's second album spend at the number 1 spot in the UK charts, in consecutive weeks, from February until April 2011?

269. True or false: Adele's sister is Lily Allen?

270. How many songs are there on Adele's album '19'?

271. True or false: Adele dated Gareth Gates during 2011?

272. Which song did Adele perform on The Late Show with David Letterman during February 2011?

273. At which position in the Argentinean Albums Charts did Adele's second album peak - 8, 9 or 10?

274. True or false: Adele appeared in the 2012 film The Sweeney?

275. At which venue in London did Adele perform on 20 July 2008?

276. True or false: Adele's song 'Hometown Glory' has been featured in the following television shows - Skins, Grey's Anatomy, One Tree Hill, Hollyoaks and Secret Diary of a Call Girl?

277. At which position did Adele's single 'Rumour Has It' peak in the UK charts - 25, 55 or 85?

278. What is the title of track 6 on Adele's debut album?

279. True or false: Adele's song 'Chasing Pavements' was a UK number 1 hit?

280. For how many weeks was Adele's single 'Rolling in the Deep' in the top 5 in the UK's singles charts?

281. In which year did Adele release her song titled 'Hometown Glory'?

282. True or false: Adele is a big fan of Bette Milder?

283. Adele's song 'Turning Tables' was written in the key of - A Minor, B Minor or C Minor?

284. True or false: When Adele was a young girl her mum made her an eye patch with sequins, to make her look like singer Gabrielle?

285. At which studios in London did Adele record her song 'Rolling in the Deep'?

286. How many songs are there on Adele's album '21'?

287. True or false: Adele won the 2011 Q Award for 'Best Female Artist'?

288. What is the longest song on Adele's album '19'?

289. Where was Adele's album '19' first released - UK, Europe or USA?

290. Which of Adele's songs was nominated for the 'The Record of the Year' award in 2011?

291. On which of Adele's albums would you find her song 'Turning Tables'?

292. True or false: Adele's single 'Rolling in the Deep' was a number 1 hit in Norway?

293. Which of Adele's songs was covered by German pop singer Lena Meyer-Landrut on her debut album 'My Cassette Player' in 2010?

294. What star sign is Adele?

295. In which month during 2011 did Adele release her video album 'Live at the Royal Albert Hall' in the UK?

296. Who directed Adele's music video for her song 'Someone Like You'?

297. At which position in the UK charts did Adele's song 'Make You Feel My Love' peak - 4, 14 or 24?

298. What are Adele's two middle names?

299. True or false: Mark Ronson produced Adele's song 'Cold Shoulder'?

300. At which venue in USA did Adele last perform on her tour 'An Evening with Adele' during June 2009?

Kylie Minogue

301. In which year was Kylie born in Melbourne?

302. Was Kylie's 2010 studio album her 11th, 12th or 13th album?

303. True or false: Kylie was awarded an OBE for her services to music?

304. What was Kylie's first single, spending seven weeks at number 1 in the Australian charts and then becoming the highest selling single of the decade?

305. Can you name Kylie's character name in Neighbours, a schoolgirl turned garage mechanic?

306. How long is Kylie's song 'Confide in Me' - 5 minutes, 51 seconds, 5 minutes, 55 seconds or 5 minutes, 59 seconds?

307. How many shows did Kylie perform in her 'Showgirl: The Homecoming Tour' between November 2006 and January 2007?

308. What was the name of Kylie's debut album, released in 1988?

309. What is Kylie's middle name?

310. Which Kylie single went to number 1 in the UK charts, released in January 1988?

311. How many tracks are there on Kylie's album 'Fever', released in October 2001?

312. In which year did Kylie first win the 'Best International Female' award at the BRITS, having been nominated in 1989, 1995 and 2001?

313. True or false: Madame Tussauds in London unveiled its fourth waxwork of Kylie in January 2007, only The Queen has had more models created at the museum?

314. Can you name Kylie's sister, the former pop star and now judge on The X Factor?

315. Which position in the UK album charts did Kylie's album 'Body Language' reach in 2003 - 3, 6 or 9?

316. What colour T-shirt is Kylie wearing on the cover of the CD single 'Can't Get You Out of My Head', released in September 2001?

317. Which two Kylie songs were on the B side of her 2003 single 'Slow'?

318. Can you name the song that Kylie did as a duet with Jason Donovan, released in November 1988?

319. True or false: Kylie hosted the 2009 BRIT Awards during February 2009 with comedy actors James Corden and Mathew Horne?

320. In which year was Kylie's single 'Spinning Around' released?

321. Kylie has achieved worldwide record sales of more than how many million?

322. What colour nail varnish is Kylie wearing on the front cover of her album 'X', released in November 2007?

323. To which position in the UK charts did Kylie's song 'Wow' peak at, released in February 2008?

324. What was the name of Kylie's children's book, released in September 2006?

325. In which year was Kylie sadly diagnosed with breast cancer?

326. True or false: Kylie is half Welsh as her mother comes from Wales?

327. How long is Kylie's album 'Aphrodite' - 43 minutes 21 seconds, 45 minutes 23 seconds or 47 minutes 49 seconds?

328. On which BBC chat show was Kylie interviewed during June 2010?

329. In which month during 2011 did Kylie tour England on her tour the 'Aphrodite World Tour'?

330. For which one of Kylie's singles, released in August 1991, was TV presenter Davina McCall one of her dancers?

331. Which song is on Kylie's side B of the single 'On a Night Like This', released in September 2000?

332. Where in the world was Kylie's song 'Better the Devil You Know' recorded - New York, London or Berlin?

333. True or false: Kylie's single 'Shocked' went to number 1 in the UK charts in 1991?

334. What colour outfit and shoes is Kylie wearing on the front cover of her album 'Fever'?

335. In which year was Kylie's song 'Can't Get You Out of My Head' released, going to number 1 in the UK charts?

336. How many of Kylie's first 11 studio albums went to number 1 in the UK album charts?

337. With which X Factor contestant, who went on to win the show in 2007, did Kylie perform whilst he was mentored by Kylie's sister Dannii?

338. True or false: Kylie co-starred in the 2007 Doctor Who Christmas special episode titled 'Voyage of the Damned'?

339. Can you name Kylie's song which is track 9 on her album 'Aphrodite'?

340. What is the name of Kylie's 1997 album?

341. With whom did Kylie end a relationship in February 2007?

342. Which record label produced Kylie's 2010 album 'Aphrodite'?

343. What colour top is Kylie wearing on the front of her album 'Body Language' - black and white, red and yellow or pink and white?

344. What was the name of the single that Kylie sang with Robbie Williams, reaching number 2 in the UK charts in 2000?

345. What was the name of Kylie's first fragrance, released in 2006?

346. To which UK chart position did Kylie's song 'All the Lovers' go to in 2010 - 1, 2 or 3?

347. True or false: In Beijing, Kylie is known as Kaili Minuo?

348. In which year was Kylie's song 'Hand on Your Heart' released in the UK, reaching number 1 in the charts?

349. Which Kylie song, released in 1990 went to number 1 in the UK charts?

350. On which of Kylie's albums are the songs 'Slow', 'Red Blooded Woman' and 'Chocolate'?

351. What is Kylie holding on the CD cover of her 1989 single 'Hand on Your Heart'?

352. What does Kylie's 1988 song title 'Je Ne Sais Pas Pourquoi' mean in English?

353. Who is older - Kylie or Dannii?

354. True or false: Kylie performed during the closing ceremony of the 2000 Sydney Olympics?

355. Which Kylie single is track 4 on her album 'Kylie Minogue', released in September 1994?

356. How long is Kylie's album 'Impossible Princess' - 49 minutes 57 seconds, 51 minutes 57 seconds or 53 minutes 57 seconds?

357. Which of Kylie's singles, released in July 1988, became her third consecutive number 1 single in the Australian charts?

358. What was Kylie's 1998 tour called, performing 21 shows in Australia and England in June and July 1998?

359. True or false: In July 1993, Kylie and her sister Dannii broke the record as the most successful sisters ever in the British charts, after Dannii had her sixth top 40 hit in the UK with her song 'This Is It'?

360. Who produced Kylie's single 'Spinning Around', released in 2000?

361. True or false: Kylie is a Tottenham Hotspur fan?

362. In which year was Kylie voted number 1 'Best Legs in Show Business' by the razor company Gillette?

363. Which of Kylie's singles won the 2004 Grammy Award for 'Best Dance Recording'?

364. True or false: Kylie was a contestant on the German version of Big Brother in 2010?

365. What star sign is Kylie?

366. True or false: Kylie is the celebrity ambassador for the 'Kids Helpline' in Australia?

367. How many episodes of Neighbours was Kylie in - 317, 318 or 319?

368. What is the title of Kylie's autobiography, released in 2003?

369. What colour top is Kylie wearing on the CD single cover of 'Je Ne Sais Pas Pourquoi', released in the UK in October 1988?

370. What colour are the words 'Tears on My Pillow' on Kylie's single, released in 1989 in Australia and 1990 in Europe?

371. In which country did Kylie's 1998 single 'Breathe' reach number 1 in the charts?

372. Which of Kylie's songs, released in June 2004, became her 27th top ten UK single when it debuted at number 6 in the charts?

373. Which position did Kylie's 1990 song 'Better the Devil You Know' reach in the UK charts?

374. What is the name of Kylie's brother?

375. How height is Kylie - 4 feet 9 inches, 4 feet 11 inches or 5 feet 1 inch tall?

376. Which of Kylie's songs was nominated for the 2002 Grammy Award in the category 'Best Dance Recording'?

377. In which Australian television series did Kylie appear during 1985 playing the character Charlotte 'Char' Kernow?

378. True or false: Kylie was nominated for an MTV Movie Award for the 'Best Cameo' in 2001 in the film Moulin Rouge!?

379. What is the name of Kylie's lingerie line?

380. True or false: Kylie gave her first singing performance in 1983 on Young Talent Time on which her sister Dannii was already a regular?

381. On which album does Kylie's song 'Step Back in Time' appear?

382. Which record label produced Kylie's song 'Better Than Today', released in 2010?

383. True or false: In 1988 Kylie performed her song 'Made in Heaven' at the Royal Variety Performance?

384. In which year was Kylie's song 'Some Kind of Bliss' released?

385. At which number in the UK charts did Kylie's 2010 single 'Better Than Today' peak - 12, 22 or 32?

386. In which year was Kylie named 'Live Performer of the Year' at the Australian Mo Awards?

387. True or false: Kylie appeared at the Plymouth Pavilions in the UK on tour in October 1991?

388. In which year did Kylie present the MTV Awards in Paris, France?

389. True or false: Kylie's 2007 single '2 Hearts' reached number 1 in the Australian charts but number 4 in the UK charts?

390. In which British sitcom did Kylie make a guest appearance as herself in 1995?

391. In which year was Kylie's single 'It's No Secret' released - 1987, 1988 or 1989?

392. Can you name the two songs that are on the B side of Kylie's single '2 Hearts'?

393. In which year was Kylie's single 'Wouldn't Change a Thing' released?

394. True or false: There is a bronze statue of Kylie at Waterfront City, Melbourne Docklands, Australia?

395. In which two countries did Kylie's song 'Spinning Around' reach number 1 in the charts?

396. Which Kylie song was released in December 2004, peaking at number 2 in the UK charts?

397. Which 1989 single became Kylie's third number 1 in the UK charts?

398. To which position in the UK charts did Kylie's 2002 single 'Love at First Sight' go to?

399. What was Kylie's 2005 tour called, performing 37 shows between March and May 2005?

400. In which 1989 film did Kylie star playing character Lola Lovell?

Christina Aguilera

401. Which single did Christina release in the US in June 1999?

402. True or false: Christina has a star on the Hollywood Walk of Fame?

403. What was the name of Christina's fourth studio album, released in October 2002?

404. In which year did Christina win the International Female Solo Artist BRIT award?

405. What star sign is Christina?

406. For which of Christina's singles did she win the 2007 'Best Female Pop Vocal Performance' at the Grammy Awards?

407. In which year did Christina celebrate her 30th birthday?

408. True or false: Christina was a contestant in the French version of Big Brother in 2008?

409. What colour are Christina's eyes, of which she also wears the same colour contact lenses?

410. In 2009 Christina became the global spokesperson for which charitable organisation, appearing in advertisements, online campaigns and a public service announcement?

411. What is Christina's official website address?

412. With which singer did Christina co-host the 2001 Radio Music Awards in Las Vegas?

413. What is Christina's middle name?

414. Which two MTV Video Music Awards did Christina's 2001 single 'Lady Marmalade' win?

415. At which position in the Australian charts did Christina's single 'Fighter' peak when released in 2003?

416. True or false: Christina's fifth studio album 'Back to Basics' released in August 2006 debuted at number 1 in the US, the UK and 11 other countries?

417. What was the name of the song that Christina featured on with Maroon 5 in 2011?

418. What is Christina holding on the cover of her single 'Can't Hold Us Down' released in 2003?

419. Which of Christina's 2003 singles is most known for its simplistic, but critically acclaimed music video that was filmed in black and white as a single continuous camera shot?

420. In which year did Maxim magazine nominate Christina as the 'Sexiest Woman of the Year'?

421. What is the name of Christina's first greatest hits album, released in 2008?

422. Which 2001 single was a number 1 hit for Christina in the US and the UK?

423. How many nights did Christina play at Wembley in the UK during her tour in November 2003?

424. How many stars out of five did The Guardian give Christina's album 'Stripped'?

425. How many copies of Christina's album 'Back to Basics' sold in the US - 1.3 million, 1.5 million or 1.7 million?

426. What is the Spanish version of Christina's single 'Come on Over Baby (All I want is you)' called?

427. True or false: Christina has appeared in the musical The Pussycat Dolls?

428. At how many beats per minute does Christina's single 'Beautiful' move - 38, 58 or 78?

429. In which year was Christina named the 19th richest woman in entertainment by Forbes, with a net worth of US$60 million?

430. True or false: Christina made a cameo appearance on an episode of Beverly Hills, 90210 in 1999?

431. Who wrote Christina's 2006 single 'Hurt'?

432. What colour outfit was Christina wearing when she performed her single 'Beautiful' on the David Letterman Show in 2003?

433. In which country did Christina tour at the end of January and at the start of February 2001?

434. Can you name one of Christina's two favourite colours?

435. Where in America was Christina's video filmed for her single 'Genie in a Bottle'?

436. True or false: Christina ran the London Marathon in 2010?

437. Which American socialite accidentally revealed that Christina was pregnant, at a party Christina was hosting, several weeks prior to announcing the news officially in 2007?

438. True or false: Christina represented the United States at the international Golden Stag Festival in 1997 with a two-song set?

439. Can you name the rapper who sang 'Tilt Ya Head Back', from his album 'Sweat' in 2004 which features Christina?

440. With which UK X Factor finalist did Christina perform 'Beautiful' as a duet in December 2010?

441. What colour shoes is Christina wearing on the single 'Candyman' released in 2007?

442. True or false: In November 2005, all of her wedding gifts were submitted to various charities around the US in support of Hurricane Katrina victims?

443. Which award did Christina win at the Ivor Novello Awards in 2000 for her single 'Genie in a Bottle'?

444. In which year was Christina named Glamour's very first Woman of the Year?

445. Can you name the second single from P. Diddy's 2006 album, 'Press Play', which features Christina?

446. Who produced Christina's 2008 single 'Keeps Gettin' Better'?

447. True or false: Christina auditioned for a role on The Mickey Mouse Club in 1991 but she did not meet the age requirements?

448. What colour hair does Christina have on the front of her 1999 single 'What a Girl Wants'?

449. In which year did Christina release her Spanish album Mi Reflejo?

450. True or false: Christina performed at Wembley Stadium during June 2011?

451. How tall is Christina - 5 foot 2 inches, 5 foot 4 inches or 5 foot 6 inches?

452. Which of Christina's songs appeared in the 2000 romantic comedy What Women Want starring Mel Gibson and Helen Hunt?

453. What is Christina's most common nickname - X-Tina, Chrissy or Chris-a?

454. For which album did Christina win the 2006 Daily Mirror award for 'Best Album of the Year'?

455. Which 2007 American Idol winner sang Christina's song 'Fighter' at the finale?

456. True or false: Christina's single 'Beautiful' was a number 1 hit in Italy?

457. What was the name of the song that Christina recorded at the age of 14, a hit duet with Japanese singer Keizo Nakanishi?

458. Which legendry singer is Christina's idol?

459. In which country did Christina live for three years before she starred on The Mickey Mouse Club?

460. In which country did Christina's single 'Oh Mother' peak the highest in the charts - Austria, Germany or The Netherlands?

461. What nationality is Christina - English, Canadian or American?

462. Which soft drink giant did Christina endorse during 2006?

463. What colour dress and shoes is Christina wearing on the single cover of 'Slow Down Baby' released in July 2007?

464. In which year was Christina's single 'Candyman' released?

465. True or false: Christina performed her single 'Hurt' live at the 2006 MTV Video Music Awards in August 2006?

466. In March 1990 Christina appeared on Star Search singing which song?

467. What is the name of Christina's fourth single from Christina Aguilera's third studio album - Oh Mother, Oh Sister or Oh Brother?

468. In 2008 Christina and close friend Stephen Webster designed what and released a collection called 'Shattered'?

469. Is Christina a smoker?

470. Can you name the Spanish title for Christina's song 'Genie in a Bottle'?

471. True or false: Christina's mother is of German, Irish, Welsh, and Dutch ancestry?

472. What is the name of Christina's fifth fragrance, released in 2010?

473. Which girl group first released 'Lady Marmalade' in 1974, the song Christina covered in 2001?

474. True or false: Christina once endorsed Mercedes-Benz?

475. In which year did Christina performed at the 'Unite of the Stars' concert in aid of Unite Against Hunger in Johannesburg, South Africa and at the Nelson Mandela Children's Fund at the Coca-Cola Dome?

476. True or false: In 2008 Christina appeared on the Turkish version of Deal or No Deal and won $180,000 for charity?

477. How many tracks are there on Christina's debut album?

478. In which year did Christina host the MTV Europe Music Awards?

479. What was the name of Christina's first fragrance, released in 2004?

480. Which rapper featured on Christina's single 'Dirty' released in 2002?

481. What is the name of the song that Christina recorded with rapper and singer Missy Elliott in 2004?

482. Which soft drink giant did Christina endorse during 2001?

483. In which 2010 musical did Christina make her feature film debut?

484. Following on from the previous question - True or false: Christina earned a Golden Globe nomination for Best Original Song in the film?

485. In 2008, at which venue in London did Christina headline at London's Africa Rising charity concert which raised awareness for finding substantial issues facing the continent?

486. How many letters make up Christina's surname?

487. Which record label produced Christina's album 'Stripped'?

488. Which of Christina's songs was on the B side of 'Beautiful'?

489. Which American comedy-drama television series that premiered on HBO in July 2004 did Christina appear in during 2010?

490. What colour hair did Christina have on her 2001 single 'Falsas Esperanzas'?

491. At which number did Christina's single 'Walk Away' peak in the Danish charts - 33, 35 or 37?

492. Where on Christina's body does she have a tattoo stating 'Xtina'?

493. Which two colours were used on Christina's single colour 'Not Myself Tonight' released in August 2010?

494. Which of Christina's singles did she promote at the finale of the ninth season of American Idol?

495. True or false: Kelly Clarkson's second single 'Miss Independent' was co-written by Christina?

496. Which of Christina's 2010 singles featured Trinidadian rapper Nicki Minaj?

497. What colour lipstick is Christina wearing on her album 'Bionic'?

498. How long was Christina's debut album - 44 minutes 17 seconds, 45 minutes 19 seconds or 46 minutes 21 seconds?

499. In which year did Christina win the 'Singer of the Year' award at the Top of the Pops Awards?

500. What was the name of Christina's debut album, released in 1999?

Answers

Katy Perry

1. 1984

2. Elizabeth

3. www.katyperry.com

4. American

5. True

6. The California Dreams Tour

7. Russell Brand

8. India

9. False

10. Firework

11. E.T.

12. Snoop Dogg

13. Pink

14. True

15. 5 foot 6 ½ inches

16. Number 1

17. Katy Hudson

18. Blue

19. Purr

20. 2009

21. Red

22. Travie McCoy

23. 2010

24. Peacock

25. True

26. Smurfette

27. The X Factor

28. 12

29. Album Title

30. Katy Perry

31. A water melon

32. Canada

33. Thinking of You

34. Teenage Dream

35. The Logie Awards

36. 37

37. Five: Best Art Direction, Best Cinematography, Best Editing, Best Female Video and Best New Artist

38. Eight

39. Green

40. Nordstrom

41. True

42. 3 minutes, 52 seconds

43. Three

44. True

45. 126 beats per minute

46. Blender

47. True

48. E.T.

49. Hello Katy Tour

50. Best Release

51. International Album of the Year

52. True

53. Sliimy

54. 3OH!3

55. 27

56. Auckland, New Zealand

57. Blue

58. Budapest

59. 'Breakout' and 'The Driveway'

60. Australia

61. Capitol Records

62. True

63. KOKO

64. Red (it is yellow on the updated version)

65. Ur So Gay

66. True

67. A cat

68. True

69. Gavin Rossdale

70. True

71. Three

72. I Kissed a Girl

73. Nothing

74. Number 1

75. Black

76. Wildfire

77. True

78. Scorpio (born on 25th October)

79. Blue

80. True

81. Circle The Drain

82. Best Male Video

83. December

84. True

85. Will Cotton

86. Teenage Dream

87. False

88. International Album of the Year (for 'Teenage Dream')

89. Bedük

90. The Young and the Restless

91.   Five: Best Female Video, Best Pop Video, Best New Artist On a Video, Best Video in English and Video Of The Year

92.   True

93.   Red

94.   2009

95.   23

96.   Johnny Wujek

97.   Greg Wells

98.   The Fight Before Christmas

99.   Four

100. Paul O'Grady Live

Lady Gaga

101. 1986

102. The Fame

103. July

104. Summerboy

105. Stefani Joanne Angelina Germanotta

106. True

107. Green

108. American

109. Four

110. 2008

111. Eight

112. Dance in the Dark

113. Judas

114. Chillin

115. February

116. 'Ralph' by Ralph Lauren and 'Daisy' by Marc Jacobs

117. True

118. Murder My Heart

119. Piano

120. False

121. Aries

122. Just Dance

123. Three: for 'Female Solo Artist', 'International Breakthrough Act' and 'Best International Album'

124. Def Jam Recordings

125. Radio Ga Ga

126. A natural brunette

127. True

128. America, in New York City

129. Left hand

130. Convent of the Sacred Heart

131. Paris Hilton

132. May

133. Bugs Bunny

134. Cynthia

135. True

136. Romeo and Juliet

137. Eight

138. www.ladygaga.com

139. Tisch School of the Arts

140. Let's Dance

141. 5 feet 1 inch

142. Born This Way

143. Ren and Stimpy

144. True

145. Elton John

146. Colby O'Donis

147. True

148. A bow

149. Raw Meat

150. One sister

151. 4 minutes, 54 seconds

152. An egg

153. Boys Boys Boys

154. True

155. Dwayne Johnson

156. Harlequin Great Dane

157. 19

158. Because she was being mistaken for Amy Winehouse

159. True

160. The Hills

161. Eight

162. True

163. Gummy worms and spaghetti

164. Lennox Hill Hospital

165. Saturday Night Live

166. Lavender

167. 2016

168. True

169. 28th March

170. Yellow

171. 10 inch stilettos

172. 2 minutes 57 seconds

173. True

174. Canada

175. Jeppe Laursen

176. White

177. The Monster Ball Tour

178. A motorbike

179. True

180. Bad Romance

181. True

182. Britney Spears

183. False

184. Wonder Woman Award

185. Hollywood

186. True

187. March

188. Poker Face

189. False

190. 7 minutes 20 seconds

191. Beyonce Knowles

192. True

193. Best video

194. True

195. True

196. False

197. Natali Germanotta

198. The Fame Monster

199. True

200. Poker Face (she also won a Grammy in 2010 for the 'Best Electronic/Dance Album' for the song 'The Fame')

Adele

201. 19

202. Set Fire to the Rain

203. Take It All

204. If It Hadn't Been for Love

205. 43 minutes 41 seconds

206. Best New Artist and Best Female Pop Vocal Performance

207. 1988

208. XL Recordings

209. Critic's Choice

210. True

211. 6

212. 5 foot 9 inches

213. www.adele.tv

214. Adkins

215. Five stars

216. Dan Wilson

217. Tottenham Hotspur

218. False

219. 2011

220. Channel 4

221. False

222. August

223. A sofa

224. True

225. 74

226. True

227. Amy Winehouse

228. Best British Female, Best British Single and Best British Breakthrough Act

229. False

230. Number 2

231. True

232. Now and Then

233. 2018

234. True

235. One and Only (5 minutes 48 minutes)

236. Beyoncé Knowles

237. True

238. Will Young

239. Chasing Pavements

240. The Roundhouse

241. The Graham Norton Show

242. True

243. 11

244. North America

245. Rolling in the Deep

246. 2008

247. Best Jazz Act

248. Bob Dylan

249. False: She won the Best Independent Artist or Group award

250. 19

251. Best for Last

252. Adele Live

253. Two (3 May to 10 May 2008)

254. @OfficialAdele

255. Best UK R&B/Soul Act

256. 2009

257. True

258. One (for 'Best Female Pop Vocal Performance' for 'Hometown Glory')

259. Save The Music Foundation

260. 2008

261. True

262. Set Fire to the Rain

263. On The Floor (featuring Pitbull)

264. False

265. Most Popular International Artist

266. Five (from 26 February until 19 March and then again on 2 April 2011)

267. True

268. 11

269. False

270. 12

271. False

272. Rolling in the Deep

273. 8

274. False

275. Somerset House

276. True

277. 85

278. Melt My Heart to Stone

279. False: It peaked at number 2 in the UK charts

280. Seven (29 January until 12 March 2011)

281. 2007

282. True

283. C Minor

284. True

285. Eastcote Studios

286. 11

287. True

288. Hometown Glory (4 minutes 31 seconds)

289. Europe

290. Someone Like You

291. 21

292. False: It peaked at number 8 in the charts

293. My Same

294. Taurus (born 5 May)

295. November

296. Jake Nava

297. 4

298. Laurie Blue

299. True

300. Hollywood Bowl

Kylie Minogue

301. 1968

302. 11th

303. True

304. 'Locomotion'

305. Charlene Mitchell

306. 5 minutes, 51 seconds

307. 33 (20 in Australia and 13 in Europe)

308. Kylie

309. Ann

310. 'I Should Be So Lucky'

311. 12

312. 2002

313. True

314. Dannii Minogue

315. 6

316. White

317. 'Soul on Fire' and 'Sweet Music'

318. 'Especially for You'

319. True

320. 2000

321. 60

322. Red

323. 5

324. The Showgirl Princess

325. 2005 (May)

326. True

327. 43 minutes, 21 seconds

328. Friday Night With Jonathan Ross

329. April (1st-12th)

330. 'Word is Out'

331. 'Ocean Blue'

332. London

333. False: the highest position in the UK charts was number 6

334. White

335. 2001

336. Four

337. Leon Jackson

338. True

339. 'Too Much'

340. 'Impossible Princess'

341. Olivier Martinez

342. Parlophone

343. Black and white

344. 'Kids'

345. Darling

346. 3

347. True

348. 1989

349. 'Tears on My Pillow'

350. 'Body Language'

351. A hat

352. I don't know why

353. Kylie (born in 1968) as Dannii was born in 1972

354. True

355. 'Where Is the Feeling?'

356. 49 minutes 57 seconds

357. 'Got to be Certain'

358. Intimate and Live

359. True

360. Mike Spencer

361. False

362. 2004 (July)

363. 'Come into my World'

364. False

365. Gemini

366. True

367. 319

368. La La La

369. Black

370. Green

371. Israel

372. 'Chocolate'

373. 2

374. Brendan

375. 5 feet 1 inch tall

376. 'Love at First Sight'

377. The Henderson Kids

378. True

379. Love Kylie

380. True

381. Rhythm of Love

382. Parlophone

383. True

384. 1997

385. 32

386. 2003

387. True

388. 1995

389. True

390. The Vicar of Dibley

Christina Aguilera

401. Genie in a Bottle

402. True (in 2010)

403. Stripped

404. 2007

405. Sagittarius

406. Ain't No Other Man

407. 2010

408. False

409. Blue

410. World Hunger Relief

411. www.christinaaguilera.com

412. Ricky Martin

413. María

414. Video of The Year and Best Video from a Film

415. Five

416. True

417. Moves Like Jagger

418. A radio

419. The Voice Within

420. 2003

421. Keeps Gettin' Better: A Decade of Hits

422. Lady Marmalade

423. Three

424. Three out of five

425. 1.7 million

426. Ven Conmigo (Solamente Tú)

427. True

428. 78

429. 2007

430. True

431. Christina Aguilera, Linda Perry and Mark Ronson

432. Black

433. Japan

434. Turquoise and purple

435. Malibu, California

436. False

437. Paris Hilton

438. True

439. Nelly

440. Rebecca Ferguson

441. Red

442. True

443. International Hit of the Year

444. 2004

445. Tell Me

446. Linda Perry

447. True

448. Blonde

449. 2000

450. False

451. 5 foot 2 inches

452. What a Girl Wants

453. X-Tina

454. Back to Basics

455. Jordin Sparks

456. False: The highest position was number eight in Italy

457. All I Wanna Do

458. Etta James

459. Japan

460. Germany (at number 18)

461. American

462. Pepsi

463. Black

464. 2007

465. True

466. A Sunday Kind of Love

467. Oh Mother

468. Jewellery: A collection of sterling silver pieces

469. No

470. Genio Atrapado

471. True

472. Royal Desire

473. Labelle

474. True

475. 2005

476. True

477. 12

478. 2003

479. Xpose

480. Reggie 'Redman' Noble

481. Carwash

482. Coca-Cola

483. Burlesque

484. True

485. The Royal Albert Hall

486. Eight: Aguilera

487. RCA Records

488. Dame Lo Que Yo Te Doy

489. Entourage

490. Blonde

491. 35

492. On the back of her neck

493. Black and white

494. You Lost Me

495. True

496. Woohoo

497. Red

498. 46 minutes 21 seconds

499. 2003

500. Christina Aguilera

www.ingramcontent.com/pod-product-compliance
Lightning Source LLC
Chambersburg PA
CBHW031601040426
42452CB00006B/375